JOIE WARNER'S APPLE DESSERTS

joie warner's
apple
desserts

america's favorite fruit

DESIGNED AND PHOTOGRAPHED BY

DREW WARNER

∾

HEARST BOOKS
New York

W

a

flavor

book

It is the policy of William Morrow and Company, Inc. and its
imprints and affiliates, recognizing the importance of preserving
what has been written, to print the books we publish on acid-free
paper, and we exert our best efforts to that end.

Library of Congress Cataloging-in-Publication Data
Warner, Joie.
Joie Warner's apple desserts: America's favorite fruit /
by Joie Warner; photographs by Drew Warner.
p.   cm.
ISBN 0-688-13347-9
1. Cookery (Apples)   2. Desserts.   I. Title.
II. Title: Apple desserts.
TX813.A6W37   1994
641.6'41—dc20   93-41265
CIP
Printed in Singapore   10 9 8 7 6 5 4 3 2 1

This book was created and produced by
Flavor Publications, Inc.
208 East 51st Street, Suite 240
New York, New York 10022

FIRST EDITION

ACKNOWLEDGMENTS

DREW AND I WOULD LIKE TO
thank all our friends at William Morrow for
their continued support for our books, especially
Ann Bramson, Sarah Rutta, and Skip Dye.

CONTENTS

FRESH AND FRAGRANT
from the oven, nothing is as irresistible, or as warmly
comforting, as an apple dessert. High on everybody's
list of best-loved fruits, apples are as popular today as
they were in antiquity. When you ask yourself why
they're so popular, the answer is just plain simple:
apples taste great munched fresh from your hand, and
they're even better when transformed into tempting
taste treats—whether that's a melt-in-your-mouth baked
apple or an apple-cranberry pie. Besides having more
culinary uses than just about any other fruit, apples are
always available. And to top it off, an apple a day (well,
make that two or three) does keep the doctor away.
Apples are packed with pectin—the same stuff that's
used to jell jams and jellies—which is extremely high in
fiber and known to be excellent in lowering cholesterol.
Apples are also low in calories, contain a variety of
vitamins and minerals, and help regulate blood sugar.
What's more, when desserts are spiced with
cinnamon—which so many are—you get an added
bonus: it's been proven that cinnamon is a potent
insulin booster, which means it helps the body process

sugar more efficiently. So, even in these health-conscious days, when everyone is busy watching calories but still longing for a luscious dessert, why not bake up lots of apple cookies, apple cakes, apple pies, apple puddings—any apple delight your heart desires? (After all, isn't happiness also part of the health equation?) That way, you can have your cake (in moderation of course) and—since apples are good for you—eat it too!

If you're almost, but not yet totally convinced, you may replace up to one-third of the all-purpose flour with whole wheat flour, or replace some of the flour with bran (wheat, oat, or rice). Use nonstick cooking spray instead of butter to grease baking sheets and pans (with the exception of the Fresh Apple Cake (page 14). Since I personally don't like the flavor of margarine and believe, as studies are now showing, that it is, in fact, less healthy than butter (of course you may beg to differ) I don't recommend using margarine as a substitute. But I do recommend exchanging plain yogurt, light cream, or frozen yogurt for the heavy cream and ice cream served along with pies and crumbles, or you may simply omit them altogether. Use common sense when making substitutions and realize, too, that the resulting dish won't be the same as the original. And, last but not least, never throw out the nutritious apple peels: I call everyone to the kitchen to

share in "cook's treat."

My collection of apple desserts includes my own creations as well as many all-time favorites—classics that I've taken the liberty of adjusting here and there, simplifying recipes and adding taste enhancers, such as citrus zest, to give a contemporary feel and flavor. And, because desserts are an occasional—not a daily— treat at my table, I'm not concerned with counting calories. When I do indulge, I want lots of good old-fashioned sweetness and richness! For those who don't consider a meal complete without dessert, but who have to watch extra calories, why not simply have smaller servings?

As you'll see, I'm not a pastry whiz—that is, I'm not concerned with creating visually dramatic "designer desserts." I believe appearance is important, of course, but I'm much more interested in eating than I am in spending a lot of time fussing with elaborate bakery decorations—that's not laziness—it's impatience! My philosophy is simple: the quicker the dish is ready, the sooner I get to eat it. That's why my recipes are as fast and as easy as my ingenuity can make them.

You'll notice, too, that the photos show it like it is—no fancy food-styling tricks here. I prefer to let the ingredients do their own thing. If the pastry is split or the cake cracked, well, so be it. And anyway, to my way of thinking, homemade desserts should look that way—

you know—homey-old-fashioned-just-like-Grandma-made-it. Let's leave the "crafted" creations to the professional baker.

When making apple desserts, I recommend using locally grown varieties. Not every apple is suited for every purpose: some are best for eating, others for cooking. Your regional apple marketing board can give you information on local varieties and how to use them. In most recipes, I've left it up to you to choose which kind to use. In others, I've suggested the more commonly available Golden Delicious or Granny Smiths, but feel free to substitute apples with similar taste and cooking qualities.

As I write, there's a cinnamon-scented apple pie baking and I wish you could experience the wonderful fragrance that's perfuming the house. Since that pie (and many others!) will be long gone by the time you're reading this, I hope you'll try these simple yet irresistible apple desserts and have as good a time making them in your kitchen as I've had in mine.

JOIE WARNER

FRESH APPLE CAKE

most apple cakes are good; believe me, this one's
outstanding. It's simple yet sophisticated, with its
chunky apple center and wonderful nutty "crust." I'm especially
fond of fresh apple cake with afternoon tea—and it's superb
with morning coffee, too.

Butter for pan
½ cup pecan halves, chopped medium-fine
3 large eggs
½ cup (1 stick) butter, melted, cooled
1 teaspoon vanilla
Grated zest of 1 large lime
1 cup sugar
1½ cups all-purpose flour
½ teaspoon baking soda
⅛ teaspoon salt
2 medium-large tart apples, peeled, cored,
coarsely chopped

Preheat oven to 350°F. ⌒ Generously butter 9-inch round cake
pan, sprinkle all over with nuts, then tilt pan in all directions until
bottom and sides are completely and evenly coated. ⌒ In large
bowl, whisk eggs, butter, vanilla, lime zest, and sugar until
smooth. Add flour, baking soda, and salt and thoroughly blend.
Fold in apples. Carefully spread batter into prepared pan. Bake
for 45 minutes or until tester comes out clean. Cool in pan for 10
minutes, turn out onto rack. Serve warm or at room temperature.

SERVES 8.

CARAMEL APPLE UPSIDE-
DOWN CAKE

d elightfully *old-fashioned, this classic country cake is quickly prepared with ingredients that are usually on hand. Replace the first ½ cup sugar with brown sugar to make it a butterscotch upside-down cake—cook only until the brown sugar dissolves.*

¼ cup (½ stick) butter
½ cup sugar
    About 2 large Golden Delicious apples, peeled, cored, thinly sliced
½ cup (1 stick) butter, at room temperature
    Scant ½ cup sugar
1 large egg
1 teaspoon vanilla
    Grated zest of 1 large lemon
1 cup all-purpose flour
1 teaspoon baking powder
¼ teaspoon salt
½ cup milk
    Heavy cream for serving

Preheat oven to 350°F. ॐ Melt ¼ cup butter in heavy 9-inch ovenproof skillet over medium-high heat. Add ½ cup sugar; cook, stirring, for 2 minutes or until sugar becomes light golden; don't overcook. Arrange apple slices in sugar mixture in one layer, thin side down and packed closely together; set aside. ॐ Cream ½ cup butter and sugar in large bowl of electric mixer until light and fluffy. Beat in egg, vanilla, and lemon zest. In another bowl, stir flour, baking powder, and salt until combined. Beat in flour mixture and milk alternately until blended. Carefully spread batter over apples in skillet, smoothing it evenly. Transfer to oven and bake for 45 minutes or until tester comes out clean. Immediately place serving plate on top of pan; carefully invert onto plate, letting glaze settle onto cake a few seconds before removing pan. Serve warm with heavy cream if desired.

SERVES 6.

APPLE DUMPLINGS

r eady-made puff pastry makes these blissful apple treats a real snap to prepare. The only trick is to seal the pastry very well or they split open while baking. But even if this happens, don't fret too much; they may look homely but they still taste good!

1-pound package frozen puff pastry, thawed
½ cup plus 2 tablespoons sugar
1 teaspoon ground cinnamon
  Grated zest of 1 medium-large lime
4 tart medium apples, peeled, cored, left whole
1 generous tablespoon butter, at room temperature
  Milk for glazing
  Heavy cream for serving

Roll half the pastry on lightly floured surface to a 10- x 20-inch rectangle. Cut into two 10-inch squares. Repeat with other half of pastry. ॐ Combine ½ cup sugar, cinnamon, and lime zest in small bowl. Roll each apple in sugar mixture to coat generously. Place an apple on each pastry square. Stir 2 tablespoons sugar into remaining sugar mixture and fill each apple cavity, reserving a little for sprinkling over dough. Dot with butter. Very lightly moisten edges of squares with water and bring dough up and twist to completely enclose apple. Press *very* well to seal. Place dumplings on lightly greased baking sheet. Lightly brush dumplings with milk and sprinkle with remaining sugar. Bake in preheated 400°F oven for 25 minutes or until pastry is golden and apples are tender. Serve warm with cream if desired.

SERVES 4.

APPLE CRUMBLE

O*f all the crumbles of all the fruits, apple crumble is, in my humble opinion, the quintessence of comfort food. I've added the zest of both orange and lemon so its got plenty of zing, plus an extra-generous amount of topping so everyone gets lots—especially me!*

4 large Granny Smith apples, peeled, cored, thinly sliced
¼ cup plus 1 tablespoon sugar
½ teaspoon ground cinnamon
Grated zest of 1 medium orange
Grated zest of 1 medium lemon
1 cup all-purpose flour
⅓ cup packed brown sugar
6 tablespoons (¾ stick) butter, chilled, diced
Heavy cream or vanilla ice cream for serving

Preheat oven to 375°F. ❧ Toss apples, ¼ cup sugar, cinnamon, orange and lemon zests in large bowl until combined. Spoon mixture into 9-inch pie plate; place on baking sheet. ❧ Combine flour, brown sugar, and 1 tablespoon sugar in bowl, then cut in butter with pastry blender or crumble mixture with fingers until it resembles small peas. Sprinkle mixture over apples and bake for 50 to 60 minutes or until topping is golden and juices are bubbly. Serve warm or at room temperature with cream or a scoop of vanilla ice cream if desired.

SERVES 4 TO 6.

FLAKY PASTRY

m *y preference for pie pastry is lard—I like its old-fashioned flavor, and it does produce the tenderest crust. Feel free to substitute vegetable shortening, or use half lard and half butter (or half shortening and half butter). If you normally shy away from making pastry, I think you'll find my recipe very easy—and it works! Just remember that the quantity of water needed will vary depending on the weather and the variety of flour used. My pastry always works for me, so give it a try my way, or, if you wish, add the ice water a little at a time until you find the balance that's just right for you.*

2½ cups all-purpose flour
  1 teaspoon salt
  1 cup (8 ounces) lard, chilled
 ½ cup ice water

Combine flour and salt in food processor. Add lard in about 1-inch chunks, stirring to coat each chunk with flour before processing. Turn machine on and off 4 times to very coarsely crumble mixture. Turn machine on, then immediately add ice water all at once through feed tube and process—turning machine off and on several times—until mixture just begins to gather into a ball—don't overprocess. Transfer dough to lightly floured surface and gently knead once or twice to form into a smooth ball. Cut in half, then flatten each piece into about a 1-inch thick round disk. Enclose each disk in plastic wrap, then refrigerate for a minimum of 1 hour and use as directed in recipe.

MAKES ENOUGH FOR 1 DOUBLE-CRUST,
OR 2 SINGLE-CRUST 9- TO 11-INCH PIES.

CRUMBLE-TOPPED APPLE PIE

What better way to satisfy both apple-pie and apple-crumble devotees than to combine the two? I often add blueberries or raspberries to the apples when they are in season—the pie looks pretty with the red or blue bubbling up through the crumble here and there.

Pastry for 1-crust pie (page 21)
4 large tart apples, peeled, cored, thinly sliced
¼ cup sugar
1 teaspoon ground cinnamon
¾ cup all-purpose flour
½ cup sugar
½ cup (1 stick) butter, chilled, diced
Heavy cream or vanilla ice cream for serving

Preheat oven to 350°F. ✍ Roll pastry on lightly floured surface to about ⅛-inch thick circle; line 7-inch fluted tart pan with removable bottom with pastry and trim edges. ✍ Toss apples, ¼ cup sugar, and cinnamon in large bowl until combined; spoon into pastry shell. Place pie on baking sheet. ✍ Combine flour and sugar in bowl, then cut in butter with pastry blender or crumble mixture with fingers until it resembles small peas. Carefully sprinkle mixture over apples. Bake for 50 minutes or until apples are tender and pastry is golden. Serve warm or at room temperature with heavy cream or a scoop of vanilla ice cream if desired.

MAKES ONE 7-INCH PIE.

SOUR CREAM APPLE PIE

add this unusual, rich, sweet and tangy recipe to your apple-pie repertoire.

Pastry for 1-crust pie (page 21)
4 Granny Smith apples, peeled, cored, very thinly sliced
1 cup sour cream
1 large egg
1 tablespoon melted butter
2 teaspoons vanilla
¼ teaspoon salt
¾ cup plus ¼ cup packed brown sugar
2 tablespoons plus ½ cup all-purpose flour
¼ cup sugar
1 teaspoon ground cinnamon
½ cup pecan halves
6 tablespoons (¾ stick) butter, chilled, diced

Preheat oven to 350°F. ∾ Roll pastry on lightly floured surface to ⅛-inch thick circle. Line 9-inch pie plate with pastry; trim edges. Arrange apples in pastry shell. ∾ Whisk sour cream, egg, melted butter, vanilla, salt, ¾ cup brown sugar, and 2 tablespoons flour in bowl until thoroughly blended. Spoon mixture over apples. Bake for 50 minutes or until filling is set. Combine ¼ cup brown sugar, ½ cup flour, ¼ cup sugar, and cinnamon in food processor. Add pecans and butter; process until crumbly. Sprinkle over pie; bake another 10 minutes or until cooked through. Cool thoroughly before slicing; keep pie refrigerated.

MAKES ONE 9-INCH PIE.

APPLE-CRANBERRY PIE

festive and fragrant, no one can resist this apple pie with its deliciously tart surprise of red cranberries. Although a whole tablespoon of cinnamon may seem like a lot—trust me—it isn't! For a real treat, serve with a scoop of the very best vanilla ice cream.

Pastry for 2-crust pie (page 21)
6 Granny Smith apples, peeled, cored, thinly sliced
1 cup whole cranberries, partially thawed if frozen
1 cup sugar
1 tablespoon ground cinnamon
1 tablespoon all-purpose flour
2 tablespoons butter
1 tablespoon sugar

Preheat oven to 400°F. ⌖ Roll half the pastry on lightly floured surface to ⅛-inch thick circle. Line 9-inch pie plate with pastry. ⌖ Toss apples, cranberries, 1 cup sugar, cinnamon, and flour in large bowl until combined. Spoon mixture into pastry shell and dot with butter. ⌖ Roll remaining pastry to ⅛-inch thick circle; place over filling. Trim and crimp edges to seal and cut 3 or 4 small steam vents in center. Roll pastry trimmings and cut into decorative shapes and place on top of pie if desired. Sprinkle 1 tablespoon sugar over top. Place pie on baking sheet and bake for 50 to 60 minutes or until pastry is golden and apples are tender. Serve warm or at room temperature.

MAKES ONE 9-INCH PIE.

photo overleaf ☞

BROWN SUGAR APPLE PIE

V *anilla and brown sugar blend beautifully with apples, giving a butterscotchy flavor and color to this homey, country-style pie. Serve warm, à la mode.*

Pastry for 2-crust pie (page 21)
6 Granny Smith apples, peeled, cored, thinly sliced
¾ cup packed brown sugar
3 to 4 tablespoons all-purpose flour
1 teaspoon vanilla
¼ cup pecan halves, lightly toasted, coarsely chopped (optional)
½ teaspoon ground cinnamon
¼ teaspoon grated nutmeg
¼ cup (½ stick) butter
1 tablespoon sugar

Preheat oven to 400°F. ∾ Roll half the pastry on lightly floured surface to ⅛-inch thick circle. Line 9-inch pie plate with pastry. ∾ Toss apples, brown sugar, flour, vanilla, pecans, cinnamon, and nutmeg in large bowl until combined. Spoon mixture into pastry shell and dot with butter. ∾ Roll remaining pastry to ⅛-inch thick circle; place over filling. Trim and crimp edges to seal and cut 3 or 4 small steam vents in center. Roll pastry trimmings and cut into decorative shapes and place on top of pie if desired. Sprinkle 1 tablespoon sugar over top. Place pie on baking sheet and bake for 50 to 60 minutes or until pastry is golden and apples are tender. Serve warm or at room temperature.

MAKES ONE 9-INCH PIE.

CINNAMON-SCENTED APPLE PIE

don't let the simplicity of this recipe—or the amount of cinnamon—fool you into thinking this pie's anything other than absolutely scrumptious. It not only tastes divine, it will perfume your house with its wonderful fragrance. Serve warm with a big scoop of vanilla ice cream and enjoy!

Pastry for 2-crust pie (page 21)
8 Granny Smith apples peeled, cored, thinly sliced
1 cup sugar
2 tablespoons all-purpose flour
1 tablespoon ground cinnamon
  Grated zest of 1 medium lemon
3 tablespoons butter
1 tablespoon sugar
  Vanilla ice cream for serving

Preheat oven to 400°F. ∾ Roll half the pastry on lightly floured surface to ⅛-inch thick circle. Line 9-inch pie plate with pastry. ∾ Toss apples, 1 cup sugar, flour, cinnamon, and lemon zest in large bowl until combined. Spoon mixture into pastry shell and dot with butter. ∾ Roll remaining pastry to ⅛-inch thick circle; place over filling. Trim and crimp edges to seal and cut 3 or 4 small steam vents in center. Roll pastry trimmings and cut into decorative shapes and place on top of pie if desired. Sprinkle 1 tablespoon sugar over top. Place pie on baking sheet and bake for 50 to 60 minutes or until pastry is golden and apples are tender. Serve warm or at room temperature with ice cream if desired.

MAKES ONE 9-INCH PIE.

APPLE SHORTBREAD TART

*S*hortbread is my absolute, all-time favorite cookie, and shortbread-cookie dough makes an utterly delectable (and incredibly easy) base for an apple tart. I think this is wonderful served as is, but you might want that extra indulgence—a dollop of freshly whipped cream.

1½ cups all-purpose flour
½ cup sugar
¼ teaspoon salt
¾ cup (1½ sticks) butter, at room temperature
2 egg yolks, stirred to blend
3 tart apples, peeled, cored, thinly sliced
¼ cup plus 1 tablespoon sugar
1 tablespoon all-purpose flour
⅛ teaspoon ground cinnamon
3 tablespoons butter, melted

Preheat oven to 400°F. ∾ Combine flour, ½ cup sugar, and salt in large bowl. Add butter and egg yolks, then crumble mixture with pastry blender or fingers until thoroughly combined yet still crumbly. Firmly press mixture over bottom and up sides of 9-inch square tart pan with removable bottom. ∾ Arrange apples in single layer in 4 rows over crust (you may have to trim apples a bit to fit). Combine sugar, flour, and cinnamon and sprinkle evenly over apples. Drizzle with butter. Place tart pan on baking sheet and bake for 45 minutes or until apples are tender and tinged golden-brown. Cool and cut into squares.

SERVES 6 TO 8.

INDIVIDUAL APPLE TARTS

e *legant—yet one of the easiest of all tarts to prepare.
To really gild the lily, offer your guests lightly whipped
heavy cream sweetened with a little sugar and let them help
themselves. These are best the day they're prepared.*

    1-pound package frozen puff pastry, thawed
4 Golden Delicious apples, peeled, cored, thinly sliced
8 teaspoons sugar
    Several pinches ground cinnamon (optional)
1 tablespoon butter
¼ cup apricot preserves, sieved into small bowl

Preheat oven to 425°F. ❧ Roll half the pastry on lightly floured
surface to a 10-inch square. Cut into four equal squares. Repeat
with other half of pastry. Line large baking sheet with foil and
lightly oil. Place squares on prepared baking sheet. Arrange about
12 overlapping apple slices to form a circle on each pastry square.
Sprinkle 1 teaspoon sugar over each one, and lightly sprinkle with
cinnamon if desired, then dot with butter. Bake for 20 minutes or
until pastry is golden. Immediately remove to rack. ❧ While
tarts are hot, lightly brush apples and pastry edges with sieved
preserves (warm the preserves if too thick to spread easily and,
only if necessary, add a few drops of water). Serve warm or at
room temperature.

MAKES EIGHT 5-INCH TARTS.

APPLE FRUIT SALAD

f*ruit salad is a deliciously light, thoroughly refined, and totally healthy dessert. Serve it well chilled in pretty glass dishes to show off the colors to perfection. For an all-green fruit salad: simply use Granny Smith apples, green grapes, honeydew melon, and kiwis.*

2 cups fresh orange juice (about 4 large oranges)
1 large Golden Delicious apple, unpeeled, cored, cut into bite-size pieces
1 large Granny Smith apple, unpeeled, cored, cut into bite-size pieces
1 large McIntosh apple, unpeeled, cored, cut into bite-size pieces
¾ pound seedless green grapes
¾ pound seedless red grapes
2 large kiwis, peeled, cut into bite-size pieces
½ honeydew melon, cut into cubes
2 cups strawberries, hulled, cut in half

Add orange juice to large bowl. As apples are cut, stir them into orange juice to prevent discoloration. Add remaining ingredients, stirring to coat with juice. Chill before serving.

SERVES 8 TO 10.

ROSY APPLESAUCE

I *like this rosy-glow applesauce just as is, but you can*
jazz it up by swirling in a little plain yogurt—or fold
in whipped cream with chopped crystallized ginger or
chunky chocolate chips.

4 large McIntosh or other red-skinned apples
½ cup water
   Finely grated zest of 1 medium lime
   About 1 tablespoon sugar
⅛ teaspoon ground cinnamon

Cut apples into wedges (eighths), removing stem and blossom
ends, but do not peel or remove cores and seeds. Combine
apples, water, and lime zest in large nonreactive saucepan. Bring
mixture to a boil over high heat, reduce to medium-low, cover,
and simmer for 15 to 20 minutes or until apples are very tender.
Push apples through strainer into medium bowl, discarding
skin and seeds. Stir in sugar to taste and cinnamon.

MAKES ABOUT 2 CUPS.

APPLES WITH CHEESE

not really a recipe, but a list of cheeses to offer along with apples—plainly one of the simplest and finest ways to end a meal in style. Use your prettiest platter to present small wedges of several different types of cheese and apple slices brushed with lemon juice, or a bowlful of chilled, crisp tart apples. I prefer a combination of Granny Smiths, McIntosh, Royal Gala, and Fuji apples. Give everyone a plate and knife and let them help themselves. Always serve cheese at room temperature —take it out of the refrigerator ahead of time—and don't slice it into wedges until just before serving or it will dry out. Here, then, are some of my favorite cheeses to serve with apples: Camembert, Brie, Port Salut, Oka, Pont-l'Évêque, Cheddar, Emmenthal or Gruyère, Gouda, Stilton, aged goat cheese, aged Monterey Jack, Saga Blue, Bresse Blue.

photo overleaf ☞

APPLE RAISIN BREAD PUDDING

bread pudding obviously began life as a way to use up leftover bread. Since then, this homey, unpretentious dessert has come up in the world and is now considered elegant enough for fancy occasions. My version uses raisin bread with the added surprise of—you guessed it—apples.

7 slices raisin bread, left overnight to dry out, broken into roughly 1-inch pieces (about 5 to 6 cups)
4 tart apples, peeled, cored, coarsely chopped
¾ cup pecan halves, lightly toasted, coarsely chopped
4 large eggs
½ cup (1 stick) butter, melted, cooled
¾ cup sugar
1 teaspoon ground cinnamon
2 cups milk
1 teaspoon vanilla
Heavy cream or vanilla ice cream for serving

Combine bread, apples, and pecans in lightly greased 13- x 9- x 2½-inch baking dish, then spread mixture evenly. ∾ Whisk eggs, butter, sugar, cinnamon, milk, and vanilla in large bowl until well blended; pour over bread mixture. Press down with spatula if necessary to soak bread. Set aside for 30 minutes to allow bread to absorb liquid. Bake in preheated 350°F oven for 45 minutes or until pudding is just set and golden brown on top. Serve warm with a drizzle of heavy cream or vanilla ice cream.

SERVES 8.

EASY APPLE TURNOVERS

*t*oo often purchased from pastry shops, homemade apple turnovers taste truly terrific. They're such a breeze to prepare, I know that once you try them, you'll never want store-bought again. You may double the recipe.

   8-ounce package frozen puff pastry, thawed
2 large tart apples, peeled, cored, coarsely diced
⅓ cup sugar
   Grated zest of 1 large lime
¼ teaspoon ground cinnamon
1 tablespoon butter
   Milk for glazing
1 tablespoon sugar

Preheat oven to 400°F. ❧ Roll pastry on lightly floured surface to 12- x 18-inch rectangle, keeping edges as straight as possible. Brush off excess flour, cut into six 6-inch squares, and place on large foil-lined baking sheet. ❧ Combine apples, ⅓ cup sugar, lime zest, and cinnamon in medium bowl. Divide mixture evenly among pastry squares; dot with butter. Lightly moisten edges of pastry with water, then fold over diagonally to form triangles. Press edges with fingers to thoroughly seal, then use tines of a floured fork to make decorative borders. Cut a few steam vents in tops, brush lightly with milk, and sprinkle with sugar. Bake for 20 minutes or until pastry is golden. Immediately transfer turnovers to rack to cool.

MAKES 6 TURNOVERS.

SPICY APPLESAUCE CAKE

r edolent of spices, this simple, old-fashioned cake may be served as is, or sprinkled with confectioners' sugar, or drizzled with warm caramel sauce. It's at its best when made with homemade applesauce, but if you choose to use bottled, do buy a good brand with little or no added sugar.

    2 cups all-purpose flour
    1 teaspoon baking powder
    1 teaspoon baking soda
  ½ teaspoon salt
    1 teaspoon ground cinnamon
  ½ teaspoon grated nutmeg
  ½ cup (1 stick) butter, melted
    1 cup packed brown sugar
    2 large eggs
 1½ cups Rosy Applesauce (page 36)
  ½ cup golden raisins
  ½ cup currants
    Grated zest of 1 large lemon

Preheat oven to 375°F. Grease and flour 8-inch square baking pan. ❧ Combine flour, baking powder, baking soda, salt, cinnamon, and nutmeg in large bowl. In medium bowl, whisk butter, sugar, eggs, and applesauce until very well blended. Stir in raisins, currants, and lemon zest. Pour liquid mixture over dry ingredients and blend until thoroughly combined. Pour into prepared pan and bake for 40 minutes or until tester comes out clean. Cut in squares and serve warm or at room temperature.

SERVES 12.

APPLE COBBLER WITH COOKIE DOUGH TOPPING

C obbler toppings are traditionally made of biscuit dough, streusel mixtures, a pie crust, or cake batter. I top my apple cobbler with a sweet, soft and chewy cookie dough that is totally out of this world!

8 tart apples (3½ pounds), peeled, cored, thinly sliced
Grated zest of 1 medium lemon
Grated zest of 1 large lime
½ cup sugar
½ teaspoon ground cinnamon
1 cup (2 sticks) butter, melted
1 cup sugar
1 large egg
½ teaspoon vanilla
1½ cups all-purpose flour
1 teaspoon baking powder
¼ teaspoon salt

Preheat oven to 350°F. ❧ Toss apples, lemon and lime zests, ½ cup sugar, and cinnamon in large bowl until combined. Spread apple mixture evenly in 13- x 9-inch baking dish. ❧ Whisk butter and sugar in large bowl until well combined, then blend in egg and vanilla. In medium bowl, blend flour, baking powder, and salt; stir into butter mixture. Using a spoon, drop large dollops of batter over apples, leaving spaces in between. Bake for 40 minutes or until topping is golden. Serve warm or at room temperature.

SERVES 10.

BAKED APPLES WITH ORANGE ZEST

*O*range zest adds a swanky note and an upbeat tempo to this irresistible variation on an all-time-favorite theme. *Lovely served warm for dessert—beautiful for breakfast, too.*

4 large Golden Delicious or Rome Beauty apples, unpeeled, cored
½ cup sugar
Grated zest of 2 large oranges
¼ cup (½ stick) butter
1 cup water
Heavy cream for serving

Preheat oven to 375°F. ∽ Arrange apples in baking dish just large enough to hold them. ∽ Combine sugar and orange zest. Fill each apple cavity with an equal portion of sugar mixture, sprinkling excess over top; dot with butter. ∽ Pour water into bottom of dish and bake for 1 hour, basting with syrup every 20 minutes or so or until tender. (You may remove apples and boil down syrup until thickened if you like; I prefer it just the way it is.) Serve apples warm with their syrup, accompanied by heavy cream if desired.

SERVES 4.

APPLE BROWN BETTY

b*etties—a simple layering of fruit and breadcrumbs—
were originally invented as a way to use up leftover
bread. To make fresh breadcrumbs for this recipe,
cut slightly frozen bread into cubes, then whirl in the food
processor just until chopped into small dice. For best flavor,
serve the betty the day it's made.*

4 cups fresh breadcrumbs
⅓ cup (¾ stick) butter, melted
6 large tart apples (2½ pounds), peeled, cored,
   thinly sliced
   Grated zest of 1 lemon
1 tablespoon fresh lemon juice
⅓ cup packed brown sugar
⅓ cup sugar
½ teaspoon ground cinnamon
¼ cup water

Preheat oven to 450°F. ∾ Spread breadcrumbs on baking sheet
and bake for 5 minutes or just until golden colored and dry.
Remove from oven, drizzle with butter and toss until thoroughly
combined. Reduce heat to 400°F. ∾ Toss apples with lemon
zest, lemon juice, both sugars, and cinnamon in large bowl until
combined. ∾ Sprinkle half the crumb mixture over bottom of
2½-quart baking dish. Cover with apple mixture. Drizzle with
water and top with remaining crumb mixture. Cover with foil and
bake for 45 minutes or until apples are tender. Uncover and bake
another 8 minutes or until top is nice and crusty.

SERVES 6 TO 8.

APPLE TOSTADAS

kids—and grown-ups alike—just go crazy for apple-topped, crispy-fried, flour tortillas. A fun-looking dessert for a party, the recipe multiplies easily for a crowd. This recipe is adapted from one in Diana and Paul von Welanetz's L.A. Cuisine.

      About 1½ cups vegetable oil
   6 (6-inch) flour tortillas
   2 tablespoons butter
   4 large tart apples, peeled, cored, thinly sliced
   3 tablespoons sugar
   ½ pound Cheddar cheese, coarsely grated
      Ground cinnamon
      Sour cream
      Grated zest of 2 large limes

Heat oil in deep heavy medium skillet to 365°F. One at a time, fry tortillas until puffed and golden. Transfer to paper-towel-lined tray to drain. (You may prepare the tostadas a few hours ahead and leave at room temperature, uncovered.) ❧ Melt butter in medium nonstick skillet over medium heat. Add apples and cook for 3 minutes or until beginning to soften. Sprinkle with sugar and cook for another minute or until tender but still holding their shape; set aside, keeping warm. ❧ Heat broiler. ❧ Sprinkle an equal amount of cheese over each tostada leaving about a ½-inch border. Place tostadas on large foil-lined baking sheet and place under broiler for several seconds or just until cheese is melted; watch carefully. ❧ Divide apples evenly among tostadas, mounding them in center. Sprinkle with a little cinnamon, dollop some sour cream on top, and garnish generously with lime zest. Serve at once.

SERVES 6.

SPICY GINGER APPLESAUCE COOKIES

*C*rystallized ginger is a delightful change from the more traditional raisins and nuts. If you want to stay classic, just omit the ginger and add 1 cup golden raisins and 1 cup coarsely chopped pecans for an equally delicious result (see photo).

½ cup (1 stick) butter, at room temperature
1¼ cups packed brown sugar
2 large eggs
1 teaspoon vanilla
¾ cup Rosy Applesauce (page 36)
2¾ cups all-purpose flour
1 teaspoon baking soda
½ teaspoon salt
1 teaspoon ground cinnamon
¼ teaspoon ground cloves
¼ teaspoon grated nutmeg
1 generous cup crystallized ginger, coarsely diced

Preheat oven to 400°F. Lightly grease baking sheet. ⌘ Cream butter and brown sugar in large bowl of electric mixer until light and fluffy. Beat in eggs, vanilla, and applesauce. Add flour, baking soda, salt, cinnamon, cloves, and nutmeg and blend well. Stir in ginger. Using rounded tablespoon, spoon dough 1-inch apart on prepared baking sheet. Bake for 10 minutes or until lightly browned; don't overcook. Transfer cookies to rack to cool.

MAKES ABOUT 40 COOKIES.

CHOCOLATE APPLE CAKE

t he idea struck me one day to combine everyone's favorite fruit—apples—with everyone's favorite flavor—chocolate! The resulting cake is incredibly moist and tender. It's delicious served plain, or dressed up with a dollop of lightly sweetened whipped cream.

1½ cups all-purpose flour
½ cup unsweetened cocoa powder
1½ teaspoons baking powder
½ teaspoon baking soda
½ teaspoon salt
½ cup (1 stick) butter, melted
½ cup buttermilk
1¼ cups sugar
2 large eggs
1 tablespoon vanilla
½ cup semi-sweet chocolate chips
2 cups coarsely chopped tart apples
¼ cup water
⅓ cup sugar

Preheat oven to 350°F. Grease 8-inch square baking pan. ∾ Sift flour, cocoa, baking powder, baking soda, and salt into large bowl. In medium bowl, whisk butter, buttermilk, and sugar until smooth. Blend in eggs and vanilla. Pour liquid mixture over dry ingredients and mix with rubber spatula until thoroughly combined. Stir in chocolate chips and apples and spoon into prepared pan. Bake for 50 minutes or until tester comes out clean (check in several places: chocolate chips will be moist when cake is done). ❧ Meanwhile, stir water and sugar in bowl until dissolved. When cake is removed from oven, leave in pan and place on rack. Pierce top in several places with toothpick. Restir sugar glaze and slowly drizzle over cake. Allow to set for 15 minutes, turn out onto rack and cool completely.

SERVES 8 TO 10.

APPLE OAT SQUARES

h*ere, simple ingredients—apple slices sandwiched between chewy oatmeal layers—are transformed into a totally irresistible, altogether wonderful, bar cookie. It's foolproof and quick to prepare, too.*

1½ cups quick-cooking rolled oats
1½ cups all-purpose flour
¼ teaspoon baking soda
½ teaspoon salt
1 cup packed brown sugar
¾ cup (1½ sticks) butter, melted
3 cups peeled, cored, thinly sliced Granny Smith
apples
½ teaspoon ground cinnamon
¼ cup sugar
2 tablespoons butter

Preheat oven to 350°F. ✷ Stir oats, flour, baking soda, salt, brown sugar, and melted butter in large bowl until thoroughly combined. Press half the mixture evenly into bottom of 9-inch square baking pan. ✷ Toss apples, cinnamon, and sugar in bowl, then spread evenly in pan; dot with butter. Sprinkle with remaining oat mixture and bake for 45 minutes or until golden. Cool and cut into squares.

SERVES 9.

APPLE-YOGURT ICE CREAM

everyone loves ice cream and this particular one is
amazingly quick and easy to make. Light and
luscious, with a delicate pale peach hue, it tastes best right after
it's made or, at the very most, just a few hours later.

4 large (1½ pounds) Golden Delicious apples, peeled,
   cored, cut into roughly ½-inch pieces
2 tablespoons fresh lemon juice
½ cup plain yogurt
   About 6 tablespoons apricot preserves
   Grated orange zest for garnish

Toss apples with lemon juice in large bowl. Arrange them in
single layer on nonstick or nonreactive baking sheet and place in
freezer for 1½ hours or until frozen solid. ❧ Working quickly,
process apples in three or four batches in food processor until
mixture is crumbly and resembles small peas, transferring each
batch to a bowl. Return apple mixture to food processor, add
yogurt and preserves and blend, turning machine on and off
several times and scraping down mixture with rubber spatula, as
necessary, until ice cream is smooth. Serve at once in chilled
dishes or spoon into freezerproof bowl, cover, and freeze until
serving. Garnish with orange zest.

SERVES 4.

GRANNY SMITH SORBET

a *wonderfully refreshing conclusion to a rich meal or a simple treat to serve on the porch on a lazy, hot summer day. The sorbet is best the days it's prepared.*

4 large Granny Smith apples, peeled, cored,
   coarsely chopped
¾ cup water
   Finely grated zest of 1 large lime
¼ cup fresh lime juice
½ to ⅔ cup sugar (depending on sweetness of apples)
   Apple slices brushed with lime juice for garnish

Cook apples, water, lime zest, lime juice, and sugar in heavy nonreactive medium saucepan over medium heat for 10 to 15 minutes or until apples are very tender. Purée in food processor; transfer to bowl and set aside to cool to room temperature. Cover, and refrigerate until chilled, then pour mixture into ice cream maker and freeze according to manufacturer's instructions. Serve in chilled dessert dishes and garnish with apple slices.

SERVES 4.